Santa Barbara

by
John McKinney

www.TheTrailmaster.com

Coast Walks Santa Barbara

© 2014 The Trailmaster, Inc.

Cover and interior design by Christian Ophus
Design, layout and e-book by Lisa DeSpain
Maps designed by Christopher Reed (GrayLightMedia.com)
Cover photo by Yen-Wen Lu
HIKE Series Editor: Cheri Rae

ISBN: 978-0-934161-54-1

Published by: Olumpus Press and The Trailmaster, Inc.

www.TheTrailmaster.com

(Visit our site for a complete listing of all Trailmaster
publications, products, and services)

Table of Contents

GAVIOTA COAST

Introduction

From Carpinteria west, the Santa Barbara County shoreline extends to Point Conception, one sandy and mellow beach after another. The coastline's southern exposure results in clearer water, smoother sand and warmer sun than other California communities. Or so locals like to boast, anyway.

These are my home shores and I'm delighted to share my favorite beach walks, bluff-top rambles and coastal hikes. *COAST WALKS: Santa Barbara* is a collection of time-tested classic walks long enjoyed by my family, friends and fellow Santa Barbarans, as well as newer adventures worthy of your time and attention.

It's been a great pleasure walking about and writing about the Santa Barbara coast. Particularly rewarding are the coast walks I've led for schoolkids, conservation groups and The Wayfarers, a walking vacation company.

Santa Barbara County offers miles of pleasant sand beach with the ocean and islands on one side and the mountains on the other. Many of the county's beaches are lined by narrow coastal terraces that have the effect of protecting them from the hustle and bustle of modern life.

Sailing, surfing and stand-up paddling are popular shoreline activities, as are kayaking, fishing, boogie-boarding and beach volleyball playing.

But walking is the most popular beach activity for visitors and locals alike.

For the coast-walker, the Santa Barbara County coast is really three coasts in one: the famed beaches in and near the city of Santa Barbara; the Gaviota Coast, ecologically unique enough to be considered as national parkland, and north county shores, including isolated beaches and a portion of the vast Guadalupe Dunes.

The best-known beaches are the southernmost sand strands, particularly the city of Santa Barbara's classic palm-lined beaches that attract visitors from across the country and around the world. Enhanced by the Mediterranean climate, Santa Barbara beaches are world renowned for their beauty and as a place to play.

The beaches back of "The American Riviera," as Santa Barbara is sometimes known, offer a great sampling of SoCal beach culture and plenty of sights-to-see. Explore Stearns Wharf and the harbor. Walk into history and learn about the native Chumash era, Spanish exploration, and the early days of Santa Barbara as a beachside retreat.

Saunter along the beaches down-coast from Santa Barbara to Montecito's Butterfly Beach, to Summerland Beach, a onetime Spiritualist community, and on to Carpinteria Beach, sometimes billed as "The World's Safest Beach." Up-coast from Santa Barbara, take a hike along the blufftops to lovely butterfly preserves where a multitude of monarchs dwell. Walk around wetlands near the University of California, Santa Barbara and and count the amazing number of native and migratory birds. Visit a World War II "Battleground," the shore shelled by a Japanese submarine in 1942.

The California Coastal Trail travels some spectacular coastline in Santa Barbara County, particularly in the county's southernmost shores near Santa Barbara and northernmost coast over the Guadalupe Dunes. While the county has the dubious distinction of having more miles of coastline off-limits to the public than any other county in California, some miles of coastal trail within its borders rival the best to be found anywhere in the state.

The Gaviota Coast, among the most rural in Southern California, is a beautiful montage of mountains, bluffs and beaches. Extending from the newest housing developments near the University of California, Santa Barbara to Point Conception this coast resembles the state's golden shores of the 19th century.

Cows graze the grassy coastal plain, red-tailed hawks ride the thermals above the Santa Ynez Mountains, dolphins swim and dive in the great blue Pacific. Only mighty waves thundering against all-but-deserted shores break a silence that is all too rare these days.

Whether you're looking for a romantic sunset stroll, a family beach walk or heart-pounding bluff-top hike, you're sure to find it along the Santa Barbara Coast.

Walk on,
John McKinney

Santa Barbara County Coast

Geography

Santa Barbara County is said to be located where Northern California meets Southern California. The abrupt turn in the coast at Point Conception is a geographical and ecological dividing line between them. North of Point Conception, the coast has a distinct north-south orientation. Pacific waters to the north of the point are colder than to the south and the climate, too, is cooler and wetter.

The southern half of the Santa Barbara County coast has an east-west orientation with a southern exposure that warms the water and the beaches. The shoreline is backed by the Santa Ynez Mountains, an east-west trending range, and by the vast Los Padres National Forest. Channel

Islands National Park is within the geographic boundaries of Santa Barbara County. Four of the islands—Anacapa, Santa Cruz, Santa Rosa and San Miguel can be seen from the coastal bluffs.

The county's south coast is dotted with popular public beaches, coastal parks and preserves. In addition, many well-signed official coastal access-ways offer easy routes to the sand and surf. Northern Santa Barbara County, by contrast, has very few coastal parks, public beaches or coastal accessways. Vandenberg Air Force Base, the private residential enclave of Hollister Ranch, and several more private holdings combine to make many miles of the coast off-limits to the public; in fact coastal access in northern Santa Barbara County is among the most challenging in all of coastal California.

Natural History

More than a pretty face, Santa Barbara's coast has an ecological significance as well. Marine life is abundant and a large percentage of the state's fish and shellfish catch comes from the Santa Barbara Channel.

Birdlife is abundant, too. With its beaches, rocky shores and wetlands, as well as its position on the Pacific Flyway, large numbers of land and seabirds, resident and migratory, can be found on the Santa Barbara County coast. Santa Barbara often ranks among the Top 3 regions in the U.S. in the Audubon Society's annual Christmas bird count with more than 200 species counted.

From a vista point on the Carpinteria bluffs, observe harbor seals basking on a beach. A monarch butterfly preserve located in the eucalyptus groves on the Ellwood Bluffs is a haven for the colorful creatures that migrate here in autumn. Keep an eye out for coastal bottlenose dolphins leaping out of the water—always an inspiring sight for the coast walker.

The Gaviota Coast is the place where the cool, moist climate of Northern California mixes and mingles with the drier, warmer climate of Southern California. This mixture creates a unique climate, one that nurtures biodiversity. Unique plants and animal species survive in the area's sandstone bluffs, canyons and grasslands. Biologists call this ecological meeting place a biogeographic transition zone and regard it as one of the most impressive of such zones on the continent.

History

For thousands of years before Europeans arrived, the Chumash, most ocean-oriented of California's native peoples, lived along Santa Barbara's shores and fished off the coast in dugout canoes. From the days of the missionaries and Spanish occupation through most of the 19th century, the coastline remained mostly undeveloped.

Lack of a safe port hindered Santa Barbara's development. Until John P. Stearns built his wharf in 1872, landing in Santa Barbara meant braving the breakers with small surfboats; passengers often got a refreshing saltwater dip before arriving on shore.

With safe steamer landings, visitors—ranging from wealthy residents of colder climates looking for a place to winter, to invalids (as they called them in Victorian times) seeking to restore their health—flocked to Santa Barbara. Health-seekers and tourists soon gave Santa Barbara an international reputation.

For the entire 20th century, the county's southern coastline was the subject of much debate among Santa Barbarans, between those who wanted to conserve the coast's natural beauty, and those who wanted to exploit the shore's full potential as a resort. Some Santa Barbarans wanted to ensure that only a wealthy tourist class came to Santa Barbara, while others welcomed out-of-town developers who built facilities to attract the middle class in great numbers.

The Santa Barbara Oil Spill of 1969, "the ecological shot heard 'round the world," had great local and even international significance. It provided impetus for changes in laws and regulations, new initiatives and programs to protect the coast and to the establishment of the California Coastal Commission.

Administration

For more information about Gaviota, Refugio, El Capitan and Carpinteria State beaches, visit www.parks.ca.gov. To learn more about Santa Barbara County Parks, call 805-568-2461 or visit www.countyofsb.org/parks/. Contact the Santa Barbara Conference & Visitors Bureau at 805-966-9222 or visit www.santabarbaraca.com/.

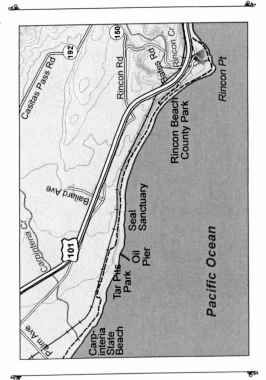

THE RINCON

From Rincon Point to Rincon Beach County Park is 0.5 mile round trip; to Carpinteria State Beach is 6 miles round trip

"The Rincon," the 13 miles of coast extending between the Ventura River and Rincon Point could be termed the Rincons, plural, because there are three indentations in the coast, separated by Pitas Point and Punta Gorda.

For surfers, the Rincon means Rincon Point, one of California's best surf spots. East of the point, surfers catch swells refracted around the point and ride them near-parallel to shore. Some of SoCal's best waves break here in a foamy maelstrom, a true challenge for surfers and skilled kayakers.

For hikers, the cobble beaches near Rincon Point, are a challenge to walk. The ocean closely approaches Highway 101, especially at high tide when waves crash against the protecting rock embankment. For many years this stretch of coast was a barrier for travelers because one could pass only at low tide on the wet sands of the beach; at high tide, the waves dashed against the white cliffs of the mountains.

On the far side of Rincon Point is Santa Barbara County's Rincon Beach Park. In 1974, when beachgoers heard the park was slated to receive a heavy dose of cement paving and other "improvements," they staged a sit-in to protest. The powers-that-be were persuaded to pave less and preserve more. Today the park consists of a small picnic area, parking, and a coastal accessway.

This walk explores Rincon Point, made by a fan delta that built a sweeping spur into the ocean at the north end of Rincon Creek. The Santa Barbara-Ventura counties-dividing creek isn't long, but it descends precipitously from the hills and, at flood stage, carries boulders to the ocean. The longshore current can't move the large rocks, so they accumulate to make the rocky spur of the point.

DIRECTIONS: From Highway 101, about 12 miles up-coast from Ventura and 12 miles down-coast from Santa Barbara, exit on Bates

Road. Head briefly south to the beach and the parking area for Rincon Point. You can also park in nearby Rincon Beach County Park if you choose.

THE WALK: Walk down the coastal access-way between the busy freeway on your left and a line of eucalyptus on your right. Head up-coast over the cobble beach, passing a number of beachfront homes that are part of the residential community of Rincon.

Pause to watch the surfers work the point, then cross the mouth of Rincon Creek. Round Rincon Point on the cobblestone beach, pass a few more houses and the stairway up to Rincon Beach Park, and reach the sand strand.

This beach-walk parallels the Southern Pacific railroad tracks, quite close to the beach here. As you stride past the tiny community of Wave, ponder whether Wave was named for its proximity to the ocean or because people "waved" at the train going by.

High tide may necessitate travel atop a seawall that borders a stretch of this beach. After 2.5 miles beach-walking, arrive at Carpinteria State Beach.

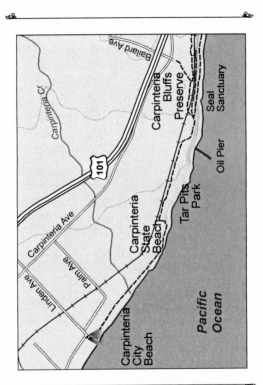

Ballard Ave

Carpinteria Ct

Carpinteria Ave

Linden Ave

Palm Ave

101

Carpinteria Bluffs Preserve

Seal Sanctuary

Oil Pier

Tar Pits Park

Carpinteria State Beach

Carpinteria City Beach

Pacific Ocean

CARPINTERIA BEACH

Carpinteria Beach Trail

From Carpinteria State Beach to Harbor Seal Preserve is 2.5 miles round trip; to Carpinteria Bluffs is 4.5 miles round trip

Carpinteria is one of the state park system's more popular beachfront campgrounds. A broad beach, gentle waves, fishing and surfing are among the reasons for this popularity. A tiny visitor center (open weekends only) offers displays of marine life and Chumash history.

Carpinteria residents boast they have "The World's Safest Beach" because, although the surf can be large, it breaks far out, and there's no undertow. As early as 1920, visitors reported "the Hawaiian diversion of surfboard riding."

Surfers, hikers and bird-watchers have long enjoyed the bluffs, which rise about 100 feet above the beach and offer great views of

Anacapa, Santa Cruz and Santa Rosa islands. The Carpinteria Bluffs extend from the state park boundary down-coast for more than a mile and were preserved by local conservationists after a two-decade-long battle with developers.

This walk heads down-coast along the state beach to City Bluffs Park, an oil-company owned pier and a small pocket beach with a Harbor Seal Preserve. From December through May this beach is seals-only; at these times watch the boisterous colony, sometimes numbering as many as 150 seals. from a blufftop observation area.

After seal-watching, sojourn over the bluffs or down along the beach to Rincon Point on the Santa Barbara-Ventura county line.

The Carpinteria Tar Pits once bubbled up near Carpinteria Beach. Around 1915, crews mined the tar, which was used to pave the coast highway in Santa Barbara County. Long ago, the tar pits trapped mastodons, saber-toothed tigers and other prehistoric animals.

On August 17, 1769, the Captain Portola's Spanish explorers observed the native Chumash building a canoe and dubbed the location *La Carpinteria*, the Spanish name for carpenter shop. The Chumash used the asphaltum to caulk their canoes and seal their cookware.

DIRECTIONS: From Highway 101 in Carpinteria, exit on Linden Avenue and head south (oceanward) 0.6 mile through town to the avenue's end at the beach. Park along Linden Avenue (free, but time restricted) or in the Carpinteria State Beach parking lot (fee).

THE WALK: Head down-coast. After a half-mile's travel over the wide sand strand you'll reach beach-bisecting Carpinteria Creek. During the summer, a sand bar creates a lagoon at the mouth of the creek. Continue over the sand bar or, if Carpinteria Creek is high, retreat inland through the campground and use the bridge over the creek.

Picnic at City Bluffs Park or keep walking a short distance farther along the bluffs past the oil company parking lot and oil pier to an excellent vista point above the Harbor Seal Preserve.

From the seal preserve, you can walk another mile across the Carpinteria Bluffs. Time and tides permitting, you can continue still farther down-coast along the beach to Rincon Beach. (See walk description.)

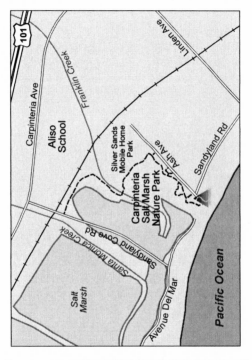

CARPINTERIA SALT MARSH
Marsh Trail

1-mile loop

Carpinteria Salt Marsh, 230 acres of a once vast wetland, was saved for development in the 1990s. Restored, with improved water quality and thousands of native plants, the marsh is now viable habitat for resident and migratory waterfowl, and a fine bird-watching spot.

DIRECTIONS: Exit Highway 101 in Carpinteria on Linden Avenue. Just before road's end at Carpinteria City Beach, turn right (east) on Sandyland Road and drive three blocks to Ash Avenue at the entrance to Carpineria Salt Marsh. Park in the small beach lot or along the avenue.

THE WALK: Check out the amphitheater and interpretive signs and meander alongside the western edge of the wetland. Turn west by a mobile home park to the banks of Carpinteria Creek. Turn around or continue along the creek.

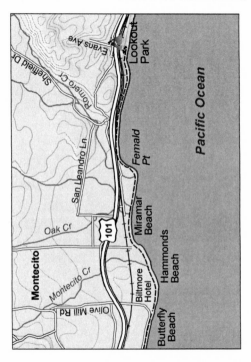

SUMMERLAND BEACH

Summerland Beach Trail

From Lookout County Park to Butterfly Beach is 5 miles round trip

Located up-coast from Carpinteria and just down-coast from Santa Barbara, Summerland offers a charming little town on one side of the highway and railroad tracks and a quiet beach below the tall bluffs on the other side.

In 1889, Spiritualist and real estate speculator H.L. Williams founded the town of Summerland, subdividing it into tiny lots and building a community/séance center. Some say Summerland was named for the weather, others opine that the name was taken from Spiritualist literature—something to do with the Second Heaven of Spiritualism.

"Spooksville," as it was known, got an altogether different vibe when oil was discovered by settlers digging for water. The first offshore oil platform in the Western hemisphere was erected in Summerland's waters in 1896. Soon, more than 300 wells were pumping oil from depths of 100 to 800 feet, an insignificant depth by today's standards but quite amazing back then.

This beach hike travels west along sandy Summerland Beach, rounds rocky points and concludes at Butterfly Beach in front of famed Biltmore Hotel. Consult a tide table and walk at low tide.

DIRECTIONS: From Highway 101 in Summerland, take the Summerland exit and turn oceanward to Lookout County Park.

THE WALK: Note the blufftop park's picnic area and a monument commemorating the first offshore oil rig, then descend a long asphalt ramp to the beach. From Lookout (Summerland) Beach, a sea wall extends 0.75 mile west to Fernald Point. At high tide, you may wish to walk atop it, but you might have to battle some brush. You soon pass a pretty little cove, bounded on the far side by Fernald Point, a fan delta deposited at the mouth of Romero Creek.

Rounding the point and approaching Montecito, observe the higher parts of the Santa Ynez Mountains on the northern skyline and the overturned beds of sandstone near the peaks. Montecito has no official public beaches, but most of the shoreline receives public use. Fernald-Shark's Cove is the first beach you travel, then Miramar Beach below the site of the onetime Miramar Hotel.

"Miramar-by-the-Sea" was a popular getaway beginning in 1900 when the Southern Pacific Railroad line was completed. The hotel, with its finely landscaped grounds and blue-roofed bungalows, used to be a passenger stop. After a century of delighting seaside vacationers, the venerable hotel was sold to a New York billionaire, who partially razed the landmark and left an eyesore for more than a decade; the current owner/developer promises to build a new high-end resort on the site.

In another 0.25 mile, hike across Montecito's third beach, Hammonds, popular with surfers. Now residential property, Hammonds Meadows on the bluffs above the beach is a former Chumash habitation and listed on the National Register of Historic Places.

Up-coast from Hammonds you'll pass a number of fine homes and arrive at narrow Butterfly Beach, frequented by Biltmore Hotel guests as well as locals who enjoy the intimate, romantic setting. Opposite the beach is the magnificent Biltmore Hotel. (See Butterfly Beach walk.)

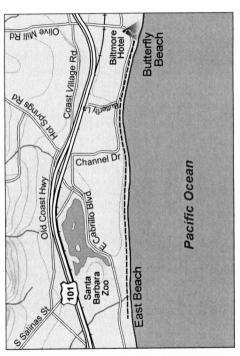

Butterfly Beach

From Coral Casino to Butterfly Lane is 0.5 mile round trip; to East Beach is 2 miles round trip

Located directly across from the famed Four Seasons Biltmore Hotel, this lovely little beach is enjoyed by hotel guests and locals—particularly from Montecito. It probably boasts more celeb sightings than other beaches, though the unwritten local rule is you act blasé and leave the VIPs alone.

Butterfly Beach is always a hit with out-of-towners so you often see locals with visitors in tow walking this special shore. This beach at sunset or under a full moon is very romantic! Weddings frequently take place on this beach and, for obvious reasons, many brides and grooms choose to have pre-nuptial photography shoots here.

Unlike most other Santa Barbara area beaches, Butterfly has a "normal" north-south orientation, so you can actually view the glorious sunsets over the water in what feels like the conventional California manner.

Veteran beach hikers may look down-coast and think something is missing. Actually something is. The "Biltmore Pier" used to jut out from the shore just south of the resort. It was destroyed in 1983 by a monster El Nino storm. Nevertheless, other coastal attractions remain and the intrepid beach-walker can walk south at low tide to Hammonds Beach and Miramar Beach, and on to Summerland.

Begin your walk by the Coral Casino Beach and Cabana Club, a private beach club accessible only to members and Biltmore guests. It's a touch of old Hollywood elegance, with a great pool and restaurant, a deck and its own entrance to Butterfly Beach.

DIRECTIONS: From Highway 101 in Montecito, exit on Olive Mill Road. Turn oceanward and drive 0.2 mile to Channel Drive, which curves around the Biltmore. Parking is scarce— limited to Channel Drive and what you can find along Butterfly Lane and other residential streets.

THE WALK: At the south end of the beach, by the Coral Casino, take the ramp down to the sand. Walk the sand or if the tide is high, the seawall back of the beach. Most beachgoers use the strand extending to Butterfly Lane where there is another stairwell from Channel Drive to the beach.

(For an interesting side trip, stroll estate-lined Butterfly Lane inland to its end at the railroad tracks and freeway. Walk through a pedestrian tunnel under the freeway then ascend a stairwell to shops and restaurants and the sophisticated elegance of the Coast Village Road portion of Montecito.)

If it's low tide, continue up-coast below the high cliffs. Above is the Santa Barbara Cemetery, known as one of the most beautiful cemeteries in the world and "The Best Last Place," as author David Petry calls it in his fascinating history book.

As the cliffs disappear, the beach opens up and you'll spot lots of beach volleyball courts bordered by a grass strip dotted with picnic tables. Continue along East Beach to Cabrillo Pavilion, which offers a café, beach equipment rentals and restrooms.

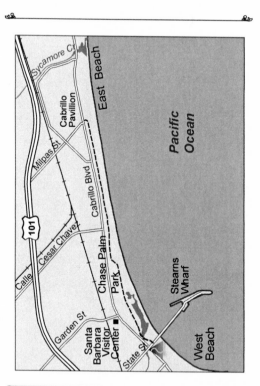

East Beach and Beyond

East Beach Trail

From Stearns Wharf to Cabrillo Pavilion is 2.5 miles round trip

It's the postcard view of Santa Barbara: sandy beach, Chase Palm Park, white walls and red roofs, the Riviera and the Santa Ynez Mountains.

East Beach is the classic Southern California beach—long, sandy and rarely crowded. It's the place to play—beach volleyball, boogie boarding, sand sculpture contests—and the place to relax, with ample square footage of sand for the discriminating sunbather.

By the 1870s, wealthy health-seekers were flocking to Santa Barbara. And East Beach is where they flocked. Horse-drawn streetcars (electrified in 1896) traveled the length of East Beach, bringing bathers from the bathhouses to the beach.

The quintessential Santa Barbara citizen of her era, Pearl Chase, crusaded to preserve the coastline. Chase and her brother Harold were honored when the city renamed Palm Park, created in 1931, Chase Palm Park.

Explore East Beach via the sidewalk along Cabrillo Boulevard (the best option on Sundays when a weekly Arts and Crafts Show takes place), along the beach itself, or with a stroll through Chase Palm Park. I suggest beginning with a walk in the park and returning via the beach.

Begin (or complete) your exploration with a walk (0.5 mile or so round trip) atop Stearns Wharf. Fun, fish and great sunset views are some of the highlights for the pedestrian on the longest wharf between Los Angeles and San Francisco. It's not uncommon to overhear a half-dozen languages on the wharf; the most-visited Santa Barbara destination, it attracts visitors from around the world.

DIRECTIONS: Begin at the foot of Stearns Wharf at the intersection of State Street and Cabrillo Boulevard. Park curbside on Cabrillo Boulevard (note the time restrictions) or in one of the fee lots on the beach side of Cabrillo.

THE WALK: Your path among palms soon leads over the mouth of Mission Creek. At the foot of Santa Barbara Street, find a plaque commemorating Pearl and Harold Chase for their civic and conservation efforts. You can't miss Skater's Point, a skateboard park. Look across Cabrillo Boulevard at the tiny visitor information center. Built in 1911, the sandstone structure formerly housed a fish market and restaurant.

Chase Palm Park is a bit more than a mile long, and popular with locals for jogging and playing soccer. At the east end of the park, cross a parking lot to Cabrillo Pavilion, where you can break for refreshments, see an art show or rent a boogie board.

Beyond Cabrillo Pavilion is another half-mile of East Beach with a turfed picnic area and very popular beach volleyball courts. A bit more than a mile down-coast (passable at low tide) leads to the famed Biltmore Hotel and its narrow beach.

Enjoy the easy saunter along East Beach back to Stearns Wharf. It's fun to walk under the pilings of the wharf to West Beach and beyond.

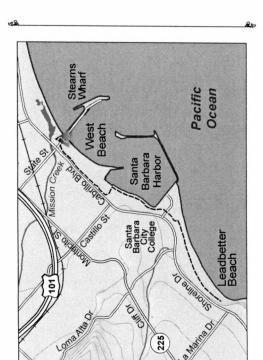

West Beach and Santa Barbara Harbor

West Beach Trail

Stearns Wharf to Harbor is 1.5 miles round trip; to Shoreline Park is 3 miles round trip

West Beach extends west from Stearns Wharf about one-third of a mile to the Santa Barbara Harbor, the beautiful home to many pleasure craft and a small commercial fishing fleet. This is a beach for sunning and volleyball playing. Not much in the way of waves here—but that's okay with the kayakers, outrigger canoeists and paddle-boarders who launch their crafts and gain access to the harbor and great blue beyond.

Begin (or complete) your exploration with a walk (0.5 mile or so round trip) atop Stearns Wharf. Fun, fish and great sunset views are highlights for the pedestrian on the longest wharf between Los Angeles and San Francisco. It's Santa Barbara's most popular attraction.

DIRECTIONS: West Beach is located along Cabrillo Boulevard, between Stearns Wharf and the Santa Barbara Harbor. Park alongside Cabrillo Boulevard. Begin at the foot of Stearns Wharf where State Street meets Cabrillo Boulevard.

THE WALK: Saunter up-coast along the beach (or on the sidewalk along Cabrillo Boulevard). Near the end of the beach, at the corner of Castillo and Cabrillo (similar-sounding Spanish street names that drive visitors mad!) is Los Banos del Mar, a municipal pool.

The beach ends at Sea Landing, a small dock that serves as headquarters for charter fishing boats and a boat launching facility. Join the walkway that leads along the marina.

At the breakwater, turn left and walk past the former U.S. Naval Reserve building, now home to a seafood restaurant and the Santa Barbara Maritime Museum with interpretive displays about local marine history and science. Continue past restaurants, yacht brokers, a marine supply store and an unloading dock for the fishing fleet.

Along the harborside walkway, note a plaque commemorating Santa Barbara's commercial fishing fleet, and a statue of a boy riding a seahorse donated by SB's sister city of Puerto Vallarta. To the right is the Santa Barbara Yacht Club.

Walk along the breakwater, which horseshoe-curves around to the east to protect the harbor, and past flags representing Santa Barbara civic and community service groups. Note: When the wind whips the ocean, saltwater sprays over the seawall and can douse breakwater walkers!

Return to the vicinity of the yacht club and walk up-coast along Leadbetter Beach, which extends from the breakwater along a little cove to Santa Barbara Point. A grassy strip by the beach hosts a popular picnic site. Snacks and meals are served up by the Shoreline Café. Above, across Cabrillo Boulevard, is Santa Barbara City College, one of the top two-year colleges in the nation.

The beach is walkable at low tide up-coast to the base of the bluffs of Shoreline Park. (On a very low/minus tide, passage up-coast is possible.) A footpath and the sidewalk ascend to Shoreline Park, a grassy strip along La Mesa Bluff overlooking the Pacific.

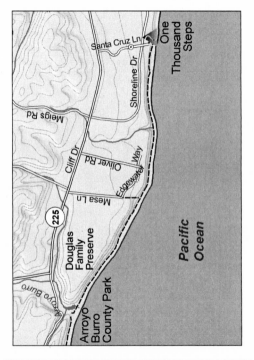

One Thousand Steps

Santa Cruz Ln

Shoreline Dr

Meigs Rd

Cliff Dr

Oliver Rd

Edgewater Way

Mesa Ln

225

Douglas Family Preserve

Arroyo Burro

Arroyo Burro County Park

Pacific Ocean

THOUSAND STEPS

Thousand Steps Trail

From Thousand Steps to Mesa Lane Stairway is 2 miles round trip; to Arroyo Burro County Park is 4 miles round trip

A long stairwell, but nowhere near a thousand steps, leads to the beach just up-coast from Shoreline Park. This beach hike explores the strand below the tall bluffs of Santa Barbara's Mesa neighborhood and below the Douglas Preserve.

The blufftop where you begin this walk is part of a marine terrace that includes Shoreline Park. Back of the beach is a hump of land separating downtown from the sea called "The Mesa," a Spanish word meaning table. Japanese farmers settled in this area and established nurseries and flower farms. By the 1920s, a Sunday drive out to the flower farms was a popular family outing. These days the Mesa is a mellow middle-class neighborhood in flux, with multiple McMansions side-by-side with funky tract homes.

Mesa Lane Stairway, the only coastal access point between One Thousand Steps and Arroyo Burro County Park leads down steep bluffs to a beach popular with surfers and other locals in the know. Mesa Lane is particularly valuable for the beachgoer looking for something a little different.

This beach walk is best enjoyed at low tide.

DIRECTIONS: From Stearns Wharf at the foot of State Street, head west (up-coast) along Cabrillo Boulevard, which soon becomes Shoreline Drive and meanders past Shoreline Park. Park in the farthest west lot for Shoreline Park or continue until you reach Santa Cruz Boulevard (not a boulevard at all, but a tiny residential street.) Park along Shoreline Drive. Thousand Steps is at the coastal end of Santa Cruz Boulevard.

To Mesa Lane Stairway: From Highway 101 in Santa Barbara, exit on Carrillo Boulevard and head oceanward (away from downtown). Proceed 1.5 miles to Cliff Drive, turn right and drive a few blocks to a rather awkward intersection with a light and turn left on Mesa Lane.

Follow Mesa Lane to its end at Edgewater, where you'll spot the Mesa Lane Stairway. Park in the residential area nearby.

THE WALK: Walk to the end of Santa Cruz Boulevard to the viewpoint. The Santa Barbara Lighthouse, located up-coast, was first lit in 1856. Destroyed by the great Santa Barbara earthquake of 1925 it was replaced by an automated light.

Descend the steps to the beach and enjoy the solitude that the sandy and cobble beach usually brings. About a mile's hike brings you to the Mesa Lane Stairway.

Expect to share the shore with scores of dogs and their owners. Along with the Douglas Family Preserve located on the bluffs above the beach, this shore is part of Santa Barbara's mile-long canine coastal zone, where dogs are permitted off-leash.

Continue another mile to Arroyo Burro County Park. A picnic area, restrooms, outdoor showers, a restaurant and more miles of sandy beach are located across Arroyo Burro Creek. The creek mouth is usually easily fordable.

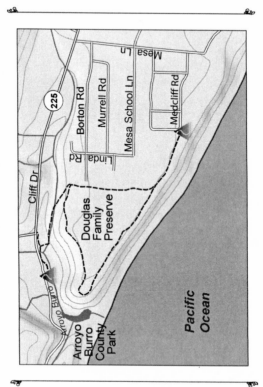

225

Borton Rd

Murrell Rd

Mesa School Ln

Linda Rd

Mesa Ln

Medcliff Rd

Cliff Dr

Douglas Family Preserve

Arroyo Burro

Arroyo Burro County Park

Pacific Ocean

Douglas Family Preserve

Douglas Trail

1-mile loop around preserve

For the walker, the attractions of Douglas Family Preserve, largest coastal open space in Santa Barbara, are many. Cliff-hugging Monterey pine and cypress trees frame grand coastal views from Pt. Mugu to Gaviota. A lovely stand of coastal live oak borders the north side of preserve. In wintertime, migrating monarch butterflies cluster in a south side eucalyptus grove.

Walkers with dogs are the primary preserve-goers. If you like dogs, you'll love the Douglas Preserve; if you're not so keen with sharing the trail with a wide assortment of canines, choose another coastal park to hike.

In 1949, Roy Wilcox moved his large nursery from Los Angeles to Santa Barbara's bluffs. Azaleas, palms, and a wide variety of decorative indoor plants were grown on the fertile land, as well as in greenhouses, and shipped to markets around the country.

Soon after the nursery closed in 1972, Santa Barbarans tried to create a park on the former Wilcox property. Developers had different ideas: a huge luxury hotel, a residential subdivision, and an upscale senior housing project known as Cypress Point. Finally in 1996, in a grand display of community support, locals raised funds to help purchase the land. Now a city park, it was named "Douglas Family Preserve" in recognition of actor Michael Douglas, who made a sizable contribution to help acquire the parkland.

DIRECTIONS: From Highway 101 in Santa Barbara, exit on Las Positas Road and follow it 1.5 miles south to its terminus at Cliff Drive. Turn right on Cliff Drive, then left into the parking lot for Arroyo Burro County Park. Park in the east lot (the one along Cliff Drive) and look for the trailhead at a gated fire road off Cliff Drive a short distance east of the parking lot.

To reach a second major preserve entry (and my preferred trailhead) follow Cliff Drive east (down-coast) to Mesa Lane. Turn right. Just before the lane reaches its end and the Mesa Lane coastal accessway, turn right on Medcliff Road and drive a couple blocks to the road's end at the Douglas Family Preserve. Park curbside along nearby residential streets.

THE WALK: From the Cliff Drive entry, join a dirt path from the edge of the Arroyo Burro beach parking lot and follow it along the edge of Arroyo Burro Estuary. Cross Mesa Creek on a sturdy bridge and ascend the oak-lined road to the blufftop.

From the main entrance, join the wide path along the cliff tops and take in the ocean views.

From whichever start point you choose, keep walking the preserve's perimeter to close the loop, or select a more interior trail. On a clockwise tour of the preserve you'll pass numerous palm trees, follow a wide path along the cliffs high (200 feet) above the beach below, and reach a dramatic vista point above Arroyo Burro Beach.

En route are numerous reminders of the old Wilcox nursery including towering bird-of-paradise and crumbling greenhouse foundations. Keen-eyed gardeners will enjoy identifying the many exotic plants that thrive in the preserve.

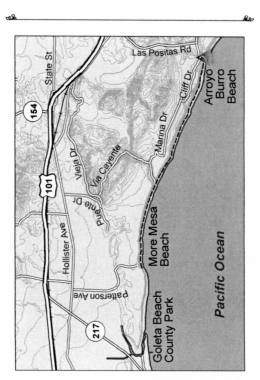

Arroyo Burro Beach

Arroyo Burro Trail

From Arroyo Burro Beach County Park to Hope Ranch Beach is 4.6 miles round trip; to More Mesa Beach is 6 miles round trip

Arroyo Burro is popular for picnicking, boogie boarding, surfing, sunbathing and beach-walking. It boasts two large parking lots and a waterside café. One of my favorite places to take a shoreline hike, it's definitely a locals' beach—not by any deliberate effort by Santa Barbarans to make it exclusive, but by the beach's location off the tourist track.

At the turn of the 20th century the Hendry family owned the beach and it was known as "Hendry's." Today some Santa Barbarans still refer to it as "Henry's." The beach was officially re-christened Arroyo Burro in 1947 when the state purchased it for $15 thousand. The park, later given to the county, was named for the creek that empties into the ocean at this point.

On the bluffs above the beach is one of the most unique residential communities in America. "Sun-kissed, ocean-washed, mountain-girded, island-guarded" was the breathless description of Hope Ranch gushing forth from real estate brochures of the 1920s. In this case, the agents were offering more truth than hype. Hope Ranch was—and still is—one of the most naturally blessed residential areas on the West Coast.

DIRECTIONS: From Highway 101 in Santa Barbara, exit on Las Positas Road and drive south to its intersection with Cliff Drive and make a right. Arroyo Burro Beach County Park is a short distance on your left.

THE WALK: Head up-coast on Arroyo Burro Beach. The area was once the site of a major Chumash village. Archeological excavations have produced many tools and artifacts. The cliffs display evidence of geological uplift; an enormous number of fossils are contained in what was once the bottom of the sea.

At (very) low tide, tidepools are revealed with all the usual common coastal inhabitants, including scores of hermit crabs and sea stars in a variety of hues.

You'll round a minor point and after two miles or so of beach-walking, pass the red-tiled changing rooms of Hope Ranch Beach Club.

More Mesa Beach follows, one of the most peaceful beaches in the county. The only public access to the beach is via the dirt path and stairway leading down from More Mesa (a mile-long stretch of splendid bluffs, undeveloped but not yet in the public domain). Be forewarned: the strand's isolation means that some consider it a clothing optional-beach.

A rocky point on the upper end of More Mesa Beach is a good turnaround point. If it's very low tide, the intrepid beach hiker can get around the point and another rocky one and walk to the mouth of Goleta Slough, large tidal mudflats that lie between the UCSB campus and the Santa Barbara Airport.

Wade the shallow, sandy-bottomed slough, resume walking on the sandy beach, and enter Goleta Beach County Park. Goleta Pier's 1,450-foot length is a nice walk in and of itself. It's a popular sport-fishing spot. A restaurant and picnic area are located near the pier.

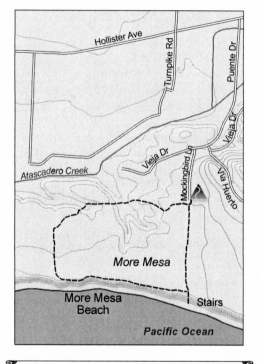

Hollister Ave

Turnpike Rd

Puente Dr

Vieja Dr

Vieja Dr

Atascadero Creek

Mockingbird Ln

Via Huerto

More Mesa

More Mesa
Beach

Stairs

Pacific Ocean

MORE MESA

More Mesa Trail

1 mile to beach; 2.5-mile loop around mesa

More Mesa offers more: a defacto nature preserve, great bird-watching, a network of walking-hiking trails and access to the beach.

The mesa was once part of Thomas More's Rancho La Goleta, who bought it in 1857 and grazed cattle here. Today, the mesa is known for other natural resources—primarily its birdlife. Look for black-shouldered kite, marsh hawk and other raptors, quite active over the mesa in their pursuit of prey. Rare birds include the northern harrier and short-eared owl.

This land has been threatened by development for decades. And it still is, though any development scheme faces vociferous opposition.

A mile-long walk up a residential street, across the bluffs, and down the cliffs on a combo stairs-pathway leads to a clean, mellow and sandy beach. More Mesa is a great walk without going down to the beach. The property is honey-combed with trails.

DIRECTIONS: From upper State Street at its junction with Highway 154, continue west along State as it becomes Hollister 1.2 miles to Puente Drive. Turn left (south). Puente Drive bends west, undergoes a name change to Vieja Drive, and passes Mockingbird Lane on your left 0.7 mile from Hollister. Public parking is not permitted along Mockingbird Lane; you must park along Puente Drive/Vieja Drive and walk up the lane past gated residential streets to the gated entrance to More Mesa. (Or exit Highway 101 on Turnpike. Head south to Hollister and turn left. Drive a few blocks to Puente Drive and follow above directions.)

THE WALK: From the main path, joined by other paths connecting from the west, cross the sweet-smelling, fennel-covered flatlands. In springtime, mustard covers the bluffs with a blanket of yellow.

At the ocean edge of the mesa is a line of eucalyptus and the dirt path leading down to the beach. Descend the steep path, stabilized by logs. At the bottom is More Mesa Beach, where sunbathers spread their towels and beach walkers can travel as far up- or down-coast as time and tides permit.

To continue the bluff-top walk, take the path extending up-coast along the oceanside edge of More Mesa. Choose from a narrow footpath at the very edge of the bluffs or a wider one paralleling and enjoy views of the Channel Islands and of the UCSB campus a few miles to the west

Continue on a clockwise route around the periphery of More Mesa. The Trailmaster likes to walk the full length of the bluffs before turning inland near a line of homes and commercial nursery. (You can also follow the bluff trail to intersect other trails on your right that lead north toward the mountains and dip into oak-filled ravines.) Turn back east, either along the inland edge of the mesa, continuing past a profusion of trails to close the loop and rejoining the main trail near the trailhead.

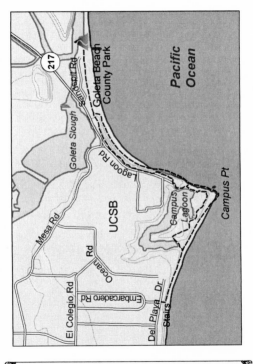

GOLETA BEACH AND
CAMPUS POINT

From Goleta Beach to Campus Point is 2 miles
round trip; to Isla Vista Beach is 4 miles round trip

Sandy Goleta Beach, located just down-coast from the UCSB campus, has a much to offer for a day at the shore: a grassy picnic area, a pier, good waves and good vibes. Lifeguards are on duty during the summer months. The county park offers all the facilities: restaurant/snack bar, fishing pier, picnic areas, restrooms.

The beach, located at the mouth of Goleta Slough, can be crossed at times of low tide to reach more beach down-coast. Slough-side platforms offer bird-watching opportunities.

A popular surf and body boarding spot on the UCSB campus, Campus Point attracts a mixture of students, faculty, families and surfers of all ages and abilities. At low tide, walk around the point to visit other campus beaches; at high tide walk over the point on hiking trails and enjoy fine ocean views as well as vistas inland over the beautifully situated university.

DIRECTIONS: From Highway 101, take the Highway 217 exit toward UCSB and the airport. Continue to road's end on Sandspit Road and bear left to Goleta Beach County Park. (free parking)

To Campus Point: From Highway 101, take the Highway 217 exit toward UCSB and the airport. Follow the signs to UCSB. Just past the entry station, bear left on Lagoon Road at the roundabout and continue on the shoreline road to a parking lot on the ocean side of the road. (Pay parking by the hour).

THE WALK: From the Goleta Pier, walk up-coast on the sandy beach, lined with a long grassy strip dotted with picnic tables and barbecues. As the beach curves south, the cliffs rise and you get the feeling of being walled off from the cares of the world. (If the tide is high and the beach impassable, take the bluff-top trails that parallel the campus access road.)

The beach at Campus Point is accessed via a break in the cliffs. Gain the point via newly constructed stairs or by ascending a dirt pathway. You can also walk the sandy/rocky beach around the point at lower tides. Also, a shoreline path with a wooden boardwalk leads along the lagoon on the inland side of the point. An abundance of options!

Enjoy far-reaching views of the coastline and UCSB from Campus Point then follow the blufftop trail as it dips into a ravine and rises out of it to meet the UCSB Labyrinth. A meditative walk from outer circle to center circle and out again is 0.6 mile.

The path dips into another ravine at the edge of the lagoon and signs inform you of your entry into a Tsunami Zone. Most hikers will walk the beach from here. (The path continues a bit farther across the bluffs and angles over to campus housing.)

Walk up-coast on the beach as far as time and tides permit. A number of coastal stairways lead up to residential Isla Vista.

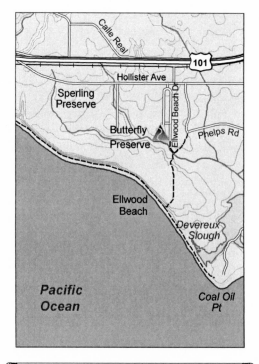

ELLWOOD BEACH

Ellwood Beach Trail

From Ellwood to Ellwood Beach is 1.4 miles round trip; to Coal Oil Point Preserve is 2.8 miles round trip; to Pelican Perch is 5 miles round trip

Around seven o'clock in the evening of February 23, 1942, while most Americans were listening to President Roosevelt's fireside chat on the radio, strange explosions were heard near Goleta. A Japanese submarine surfaced off the rich oil field on Ellwood Beach, 12 miles up-coast from Santa Barbara, and lobbed sixteen shells into the tidewater field and at the Coast Highway bridge over the Southern Pacific tracks.

Tokyo claimed the raid "a great military success" though the marksmen inflicted only $500 worth of damage. A plaque near the Bacara Resort (see Haskell's Beach walk) commemorates the event, the first attack on the American mainland since the War of 1812.

The walk across Ellwood bluffs and beach is interesting for more than historical reasons. Visit a beach popular with the UCSB community and local surfers, encounter sand dunes, a snowy plover preserve and the Devereux Slough, a unique intertidal ecosystem protected by Coal Oil Point Preserve.

DIRECTIONS: From Highway 101 in Goleta, exit on Storke Road/Glen Annie and head south to Hollister Avenue. Turn right and drive 0.9 mile to signed "Entrance Road" and turn left to immediately hit a T-junction where you'll make another left on Ellwood Beach Drive, which curves right and passes long rows of apartments and dead-ends in a half mile at a green gate. Find street parking and begin on the dirt path to the left of the gate.

THE WALK: Follow the path along a line of eucalyptus, dipping into a ravine, crossing wet bottomland on a plank and rising again to the Ellwood bluffs. At a fork, a wide path leads right toward the monarch butterfly groves.

The path to Ellwood stays to the right (west) side of the eucalyptus windbreak. About 0.6 mile from the start, the reach the edge of the bluffs.

Descend to Ellwood Beach on paths leading down the low cliffs.

Walk down-coast on the beach bordered by low dunes, along with a great deal of fenced-off habitat for the snowy plover. Take the short path up to Coal Oil Point, anchoring the east side of the slough, to interpretive displays and a vista point.

You can continue down-coast to the Isla Vista beaches (See Goleta Beach/Campus Point walk description), but to see more of Ellwood Beach, retrace your steps up-coast to where you accessed the beach and continue walking.

Wooden pilings and supports lining the base of the cliffs suggest you're trekking the former Ellwood Oil Field/World War II "Battlefield." A mile's walk leads to a formerly private pier that supported oil-drilling operations. When drilling ceased in 1958, cormorants and brown pelicans began roosting on the pier's old pilings; in 2005, when the pier was removed, four above-water platforms were fashioned as roosts for the birds. Below-surface pilings serve as an artificial reef.

Another half-mile of walking leads to Haskell's Beach/Bacara Resort and Spa.

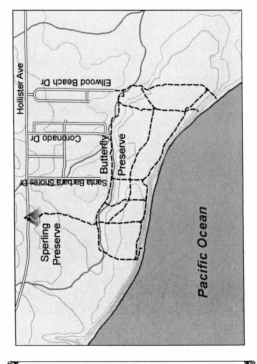

Hollister Ave

Ellwood Beach Dr

Coronado Dr

Santa Barbara Shores Dr

Butterfly Preserve

Sperling Preserve

Pacific Ocean

SANTA BARBARA SHORES

Santa Barbara Shores Trail

3.5-mile loop; longer and shorter options available

Santa Barbara Shores Park/Sperling Preserve is a mosaic of grassland, vernal pools and some of the nation's best Monarch butterfly groves—all linked with an enticing network of footpaths that serve up stunning views of the Santa Ynez Mountains, Channel Islands and wide blue Pacific.

A half-mile wide grassland extends to the edge of the sea cliffs. In winter and spring, the various grasses are a palette of greens dotted with shallow, shimmering pools. In summer and autumn, the grasses turn shades of amber gold and russet.

Monarch butterflies migrate to winter roosts in the eucalyptus woodlands that border the inland side of Santa Barbara Shores. Scientists rate these groves as among the three largest overwintering sites west of the Rockies. One leg of this favorite loop hike explores Ellwood's main monarch grove and adjacent Coronado Butterfly Preserve.

The bluffs have an excellent, though mostly unsigned, trail system. For a first-time visit, I'd suggest a counter-clockwise loop out to the coast and a return via the butterfly groves.

DIRECTIONS: From Highway 101, some 12 miles upcoast from downtown Santa Barbara, take the Glen Annie Road/Storke Road exit. Turn left on Storke Road and drive to the first intersection. Turn right on Hollister Avenue and proceed 1.6 miles to the signed entrance for Santa Barbara Shores and a good-sized parking lot.

THE HIKE: Join the wide, major trail that leads toward the ocean. The path splits and you can either dip in and out of a ravine or skirt the edge of a ravine on a narrow footpath. Bear right and proceed to the eucalyptus windbreak and east boundary of Sandpiper Golf Course.

Here you'll turn left and head shoreward, dipping in and out of another ravine following the edge of the golf course to intersect a bluff edge trail about 0.6 mile from the trailhead.

Head down-coast atop the 60 to 80-foot high cliffs, cloaked in buckwheat, sage, lemonade berry, mustard and fennel. After 0.75 mile of travel reach a junction with a major beach access trail. (You can walk this beach to the university, but beware that it's among the state's tar-iest and you won't get far before black goo gloms onto your shoes.)

Continue another 0.25 mile across the bluffs to a line of eucalyptus trees and join a north-trending trail that follows the trees inland. The view to the right (east) is dominated by two towers—UCSB's 175-foot Storke Tower, tallest structure in Santa Barbara County, and Santa Barbara Airport's control tower.

As you near the residential area of Santa Barbara Shores, you'll encounter a confusion of paths meandering amidst the eucalyptus. Head toward the end of these residential cul-de-sacs and a bit to your left (west) until you intersect the major east-west footpath through the euca-lyptus groves/Monarch butterfly preserve. Head left on this path through butterfly country, over a forest floor strewn with thick layers of bark and leaves. Emerging from the eucalyptus, you'll intersect the main trail that will return you to the trailhead.

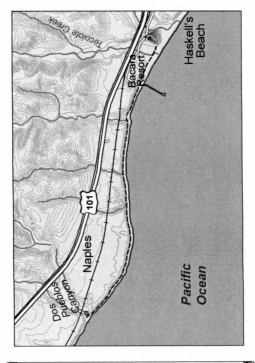

HASKELL'S BEACH AND BACARA RESORT

Haskell's Beach Trail

From Bacara Resort to Dos Pueblos Canyon is 5.5 miles round trip

For decades, Haskell's was a locals-only beach, a secret surf spot, off the Santa Barbara tourist track and far from its many restaurants and hotels. All that changed in 2001 when the beach became a backdrop for the internationally marketed, high-end Bacara Resort and Spa.

Today, Haskell's/Bacara Beach is frequented by guests at the stunning, Spanish Revival-style resort and by locals who come to surf, play and walk along a shoreline that's been public for generations. From a public parking lot (free), a footpath leads to the beach, restrooms, outdoor showers, and a little picnic area.

A great beach hike awaits. Stride up-coast from the resort to a deserted, mostly undeveloped coastline. Squadrons of pelicans rest on the reefs and swoop low over the water. Harbor seals haul out on the beach for a snooze.

Two warnings for beach hikers: Consult a local tide table and walk at low tide. And beware of dabs and globs of tar on the rocks and sand.

DIRECTIONS: From northbound Highway 101. Some 12 miles up-coast from downtown Santa Barbara, exit on Storke Road and go left 0.4 mile to Hollister Avenue. Turn right (west) and drive 2 miles. Veer left toward the entrance of the Sandpiper Golf Course onto the Bacara Resort access road and proceed 0.5 mile. Turn left at the beach access sign and into the public parking area above the beach.

THE WALK: Descend a wide path from the parking lot to the beach. Head up-coast and soon cross the shallow mouth of Tecolote Creek. Sycamore, oak, cottonwood and willow line the banks of the creek, which meanders down the coastal slopes of the Santa Ynez Mountains. A brackish lagoon is habitat for the Southwestern pond turtle.

Pass below the resort, which looks a bit like a giant wedding cake from the beach hiker's point of view, and reach the Venoco Pier, private property and off-limits to beach hikers. (Venoco's Ellwood Plant, an oil-and-gas-processing facility located just down the road from the resort, is not visible from the beach, but it is an appallingly ugly greeting to beach- and Bacara-bound motorists, despite the resort's efforts to landscape it out of view.)

Not far up-coast from the pier, round a little cove and reach a hundred yard-long series of rock reefs. Tide pools lie hidden in what resemble long, narrow and very shallow gullies.

About a mile from the resort, the beach opens up and it's easy to feel like you're the only one around for miles; on a weekday that might very well be the case! Fluted cliff bottoms have some cave-like recesses where you can find shade or a picnic spot out of the wind.

Trail's end for all but the most intrepid beach hikers is the creek flowing through Dos Pueblos Canyon to the ocean. For many generations the native Chumash had villages here. It's a nice place to relax before heading back down-coast.

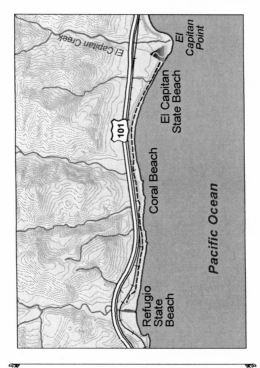

El Capitan Creek

El Capitan Point

El Capitan State Beach

101

Coral Beach

Pacific Ocean

Refugio State Beach

EL CAPITAN AND REFUGIO STATE BEACHES

El Capitan Beach Trail

From El Capitan to Refugio State Beach is 6 miles round trip

Beach, bluff and bike trails link El Capitan and Refugio State Beaches. Depending on the tide, you can usually walk up-coast along El Capitan Beach as far as Coral Canyon Beach. Join bluff trails or a sketchy bike path for the balance of the walk to Refugio Beach.

A long staircase leads to a narrow beach at the mouth of El Capitan Creek, popular with swimmers and boogie-boarders. And with surfers, too, when conditions are right at El Capitan Point.

Monarch butterflies over-winter in the trees along El Capitan Creek. The popular campground is always filled on the weekends and weekdays during the warmer months.

"El Capitan" refers to Captain Jose Francisco de Ortega, a Spanish Army officer who served as trail scout for the Portola expedition. When he retired in 1795, he owed the army money and offered to square things by raising cattle. The government granted him a 25-mile long coastal strip extending from just east of Pt. Conception to Refugio Canyon. He called his land *Nuestra Senora del Refugio*, "Our Lady of Refuge." Alas, Captain Ortega's retirement was short-lived; he died three years later and was buried at the Santa Barbara Mission.

Refugio State Beach is a combo of sand and rocky shore with tide pools. Swimming and kayaking are favorite activities here—along with camping in the popular campground. Visitors love the tropical isle feel of the sleepy lagoon at the mouth of Refugio Creek and the picnic ground under the palms.

El Capitan and Refugio are popular beach campgrounds and nice places to spend a weekend. Each beach boasts a small camp store (open summer days and weekends only during other seasons), so refreshments are available on both ends of your beach walk.

DIRECTIONS: From Highway 101, 19 miles up-coast from Santa Barbara, take the El Capitan State Beach exit. Park in one of the day use areas; the park day use fee is also honored at Refugio and Gaviota State Beaches.

THE WALK: Descend one of the paths or staircases to the shore and head up-coast along the mixed sandy and rocky beach. Sea cliffs are steep here. You'll pass wide Coral Canyon, its walls covered with beds of highly deformed light-colored shales.

At Coral Beach, tides often discourage beach-walking, so head up to the bluffs and follow the bike path. The bike path (long officially closed to bikes due to a severely eroded section) is passable for pedestrians.

On the approach to Refugio State Beach, look for abundant kelp just offshore. If a breeze is blowing over the water, note how areas with kelp are smooth and kelp-less areas are rippled.

Refugio State Beach, at the mouth of Refugio Canyon, is a rocky beach with tidepools. Turn around here, or continue up-coast (it's 10 more miles to Gaviota State Beach) for as long as time and tides permit.

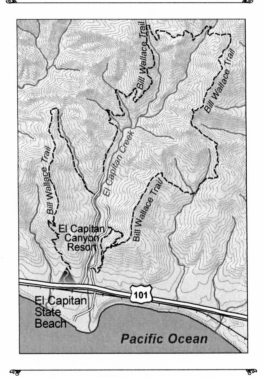

El Capitan Canyon Resort

El Capitan State Beach

Pacific Ocean

Bill Wallace Trail

El Capitan Creek

101

El Capitan Canyon

Canyon and Ridgetop Trails

2 to 5 miles or more round trip

El Capitan Canyon offers nature lodging and hiking trails on 300 hilly acres overlooking the ocean. The camp features deluxe safari tents and cozy cabins with beds, linens and bathrooms.

Most people come to relax and are more apt to walk or ride a beach cruiser to the nearby beach rather than hike in the hills; hikers, however, can enjoy walking miles of old ranch roads on the property.

DIRECTIONS: From Santa Barbara, drive 18 miles up-coast on Highway 101. Take the El Capitan State Beach exit and turn inland, following signs to El Capitan Canyon.

THE WALK: Paths lead alongside El Capitan Creek and ascend the ridges above El Capitan Canyon for stunning views of the Gaviota Coast, Pacific Ocean and Santa Ynez Mountains.

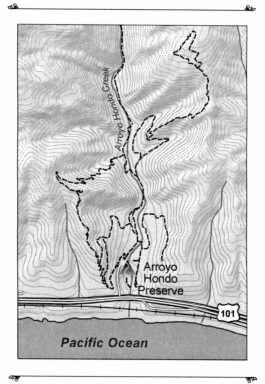

Arroyo Hondo Creek

Arroyo Hondo Preserve

101

Pacific Ocean

ARROYO HONDO PRESERVE

Creek, West Ridge, Outlaw Trails

2 to 5 mile loops, plus guided nature hikes

A deep sandstone gorge cut by the Arroyo Hondo "Deep Stream" is the highlight of this preserve, located up-coast from Santa Barbara between Refugio State Beach and Gaviota State Park.

Arroyo Hondo Preserve is managed by The Land Trust for Santa Barbara County, which coordinater fund-raising efforts to purchase the 782-acre Arroyo Hondo Ranch from rancher J.J. Hollister and co-owners in 2001.

The preserve rises some 3,000 feet in elevation from the Pacific to the upper slopes of the Santa Ynez Mountains in Los Padres National Forest. Hiking opportunities range in difficulty from easy to strenuous in Arroyo Hondo, sometimes termed a "Little Yosemite" for the look of its steep-walled gorge.

Arroyo Hondo is steeped in history. Evidence of a Chumash village, estimated to be 5,000 years old, lies near the creek. Ancient grape vines gone wild twist their tendrils among creekside sycamores. One old trail in the preserve dates to the early 19th century when Chumash and padres used it to travel from the coast to Mission Santa Ynez.

California history buffs will be intrigued by a visit to the historic adobe, built in 1842 by descendants of Jose Francisco de Ortega, first commandante of Santa Barbara's Presidio. Later in the 19th century, the adobe served as a stage stop.

The relatively pristine Arroyo Hondo is habitat for the endangered steelhead trout. Other endangered species found in the preserve include the peregrine falcon, tidewater goby and California red-legged frog.

Arroyo Hondo Preserve is open free to the public, by reservation only, on the first and third weekends of the month. For more information about Arroyo Hondo Preserve or to make a reservation to visit, call 805-567-1115 or email arroyohondo@sblandtrust.org. Inquire about the regularly scheduled docent-led nature hikes.

DIRECTIONS: From Highway 101, about 5 miles up-coast past the Refugio State Beach exit, look for Call Box #101-402; slow as you approach Call Box #101-412 and make a sharp right turn from the highway onto the Preserve driveway. Follow the driveway over a bridge to a parking area by a barn. To return Santa Barbara: From the top of the driveway, carefully make a right turn onto the highway, drive 3 miles, and exit at Mariposa Reina. Go over the bridge and take the Highway 101 southbound onramp.

THE WALK: The Trailmaster suggests first-time visitors join the guided interpretive walk, which leads to the mouth of Arroyo Hondo Creek, where efforts are underway to restore the steelhead trout population. Historical highlights include the Ortega Adobe and colorful tales of the outlaws who used the canyon as a hideout.

After the guided tour, wander down to the estuary and walk the beach or take a hike in the hills. Fashion loops of 2 to 5 miles on the well-marked trail system that includes creekside paths and old ranch roads. Upper Outlaw Trail offers inspiring mountain vistas. Relax in Hollister Meadow, which hosts a shady picnic area.

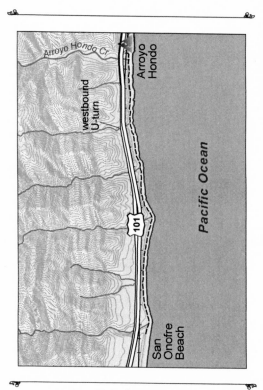

Arroyo Honda Cr

Arroyo Hondo

westbound U-turn

101

Pacific Ocean

San Onofre Beach

ARROYO HONDO TRESTLES

Coastal Trail

From Arroyo Hondo Trestles to San Onofre Beach is 6 miles round trip

The 2.5 miles walk east to Tajiguas Beach is also a pleasant excursion

"A quarter mile from the highway and a world apart."

That's a good way to describe the Gaviota Coast in general and the 6-mile length of shore from the mouth of Arroyo Hondo Creek to Gaviota State Park in particular. A decade ago, when conservationists advanced the notion of "Gaviota Coast National Seashore" this is the kind of seashore they thought worthy of consideration as national parkland.

A great place to begin exploration of this wild coast is at Arroyo Hondo Vista Point. Savor ocean and island views from the blufftop or from a vintage Coast Highway bridge (closed to vehicles). Trains rumbling across the high trestles over Arroyo Hondo are an impressive sight.

This walk begins with a descent of Arroyo Hondo to the beach and heads west around a series of points to San Onofre Beach. Depending on the season and sand deposition, this beach can either be rather rocky or a beautiful half-mile sand strand.

San Onofre Beach is the most "popular" beach on the Gaviota Coast, though I've never spotted more than 20 people using it, and often I've crossed it without seeing anyone at all. Note that it has the rep of being "clothing optional."

But this is walk is truly about the journey not the destination. Make it a 6-mile one-way journey to Gaviota State Beach by arranging a car shuttle. Be sure to walk this shore at low tide, the lower the better.

DIRECTIONS: (If you know the correct left turn lane you can make a U-turn from westbound 101 (toward Gaviota) to eastbound 101 (back toward Santa Barbara). Safest way to go: From Highway 101 in Santa Barbara head up-coast (west) about 29 miles to Mariposa La

Reina turnoff. Continue past an oil processing facility, then get back on the highway heading down-coast and travel 4 miles to the signed "Vista Point" exit and to roadside parking. (Parking for San Onofre Beach, end point for this hike, is located 1.2 miles down-coast from the Mariposa La Reina exit.)

THE WALK: Walk down toward the old Highway 101 bridge, bear left on a pathway just before the bridge, cross the railroad tracks, and descend into the canyon on concrete steps under the trestle. Descend the trail to the boulder-strewn, driftwood-littered mouth of the creek.

Head west with the ocean blue to the south and nearly vertical, upturned shale formations soaring high overhead to the north.

Walk into the heart of Gaviota-Land, past a series of small coves and rocky ledges. Sometimes you'll see a solitary angler perched on a point but don't be surprised if you have a beach to yourself. Pick your way 100 yards or so over rocky shore to reach San Onofre Beach. Remember those high shale cliffs and the rising tide and plan your return accordingly.

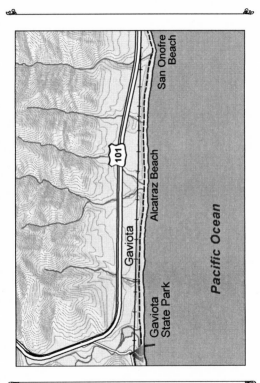

San Onofre Beach

101

Alcatraz Beach

Gaviota

Pacific Ocean

Gaviota State Park

GAVIOTA COAST

Gaviota Coast Trail

From Gaviota State Beach to Vista del Mar is 5 miles round trip; to San Onofre Beach is 6 miles round trip

Railroad trestles tower over Gaviota Beach and the usually crowded state park campground located at a 90-degree bend in the road—where east-west trending Highway 101 turns north. A train rumbling over the high trestles is an impressive sight.

Swimming, picnicking and surf fishing are popular activities at this mellow sand strand located 30 miles up-coast from Santa Barbara. Walk out onto the historic fishing pier, which includes a hoist to get boats in and out of the water.

The rural Gaviota Coast is a magnificent blend of beaches and bluffs. Cows graze the grassy coastal plain, red-tailed hawks ride the thermals above the Santa Ynez Mountains, dolphins swim and dive in the great blue Pacific. Only mighty waves thundering against all-but-deserted shores break a silence that is all too rare in Southern California. Conservationists once even proposed a "Gaviota National Seashore," to protect this coast and the mountains back of it—though the notion never gained much political support.

Gaviota coast-walking is best done at low tide. (In some places strategic retreat is possible via intermittent cliff-side paths and careful passage along the railroad tracks.)

With favorable tides and by making car shuttle arrangements, you can make one-way jaunts to Gaviota's gems: 3 miles to San Onofre Beach; 6 miles to the old highway bridge and Arroyo Hondo Trestles (Vista Point); 10 miles one way to Refugio State Beach.

The Trailmaster strongly recommends first driving to Gaviota State Park, then driving down-coast to access Gaviota beaches. Legal left turns from westbound Highway 101 are few and far between and not for the faint-hearted. The beaches (small signs, limited parking) are much easier to spot when driving down-coast.

DIRECTIONS: From Santa Barbara, drive up-coast (west) some 30 miles on Highway 101. Just as the highway makes a dramatic bend north, you'll spot a sign for Gaviota State Park. Merge left into the left turn lane and carefully turn left across the highway onto the state park entry road. The park road leads to a kiosk, then down to the beach.

THE WALK: Survey the shoreline scene from Gaviota Pier and head down-coast. Unless its low tide, passage can be a challenging. Bluffs crowd the shoreline, narrowing the beach. Unless it's low tide, it's necessary to negotiate several ledges and clamber over rocks to avoid the surf.

The Spanish explorers who marched by in 1769 and named this coast La Gaviota (Seagull) got it right. Gulls and many varieties of shore-birds populate the beaches.

In 2.5 miles reach Vista Del Mar, a secluded quarter-mile long strand. A narrow trail leads up to the bluffs, marked by a state park sign.

This beach hike's destination, half-mile long San Onofre Beach is next en route. Heads-up: this beach is known to be "clothing optional" in summer for a small number of nudists and "sand optional" in winter after storms and high surf scour away the beach.

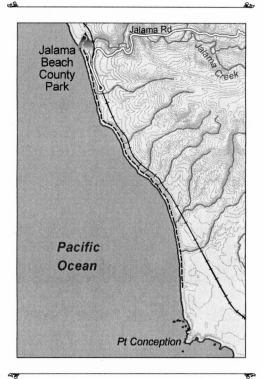

Jalama Rd

Jalama Creek

Jalama
Beach
County
Park

Pacific
Ocean

Pt Conception

JALAMA BEACH AND PT. CONCEPTION

De Anza Trail

From Jalama County Park to just-short of Pt. Conception is 10 miles round trip

Surfers, wind surfers and surf fisherman have claimed this remote, windswept beach. Jalama wins the prize for the Southern California beach located the farthest from Highway 1.

The beach is known to be notoriously tar-covered, but that does not dissuade regulars who frequent the popular campground. Try the famed Jalama Burger at the camp store/snack bar.

At Pt. Conception, the western-trending shoreline of Southern California turns sharply northward and heralds a number of changes: a colder Pacific, foggier days, cooler air. Pt. Conception serves as a line of ecological demarcation between differing marine life occupying the two sections, including species of polyps, abalone, crabs and limpets. Climatically, geographically and sociologically, it can be argued that Southern California ends at Pt. Conception.

From Jalama County Park, the only genuinely public access point anywhere near Point Conception, you can explore a pristine length of beach. If the tide is right (consult a tide table), you can walk to within about a half-mile of the Point. You'll follow in the footsteps of the De Anza Expedition of 1775-76 that brought 240 colonists from Mexico up the coast to found the city of San Francisco.

Be warned that the Bixby Ranch and Hollister Ranch are private property holders with a dim view of coastal access and coastal trails. Remember: keep to the beach and don't follow inland trails onto ranch land.

DIRECTIONS: Jalama County Park is located 20 miles southwest of Lompoc off Highway 1. From Highway 101, near Gaviota, exit on Highway 1 north and proceed 14 miles to Jalama Road. Turn left and go 14 more miles through some beautiful ranch country to the county park.

THE WALK: Meander over the low dunes and head down-coast. The park includes only about 0.5 mile of shoreline, so you soon walk beyond the park boundary. The sandy beach narrows and gives way to rockier shore. Offshore, on the rocky reefs, seals linger. Hint: the smooth tops of sea walls make a good trail if high tides force a retreat inland.

Occasionally, Southern Pacific railroad tracks come into view; with the crashing of the breakers, you can barely hear passing trains. Because no public roads extend along this section of coast, walking or looking out a train window are the only ways to see this special country. Halfway through this walk, after some lazy bends, the coastline extends almost due south, and the Pt. Conception Coast Guard Reservation comes into view.

A bit more than 0.5 mile from the lighthouse, you'll run out of beach to walk; passage is blocked by waves crashing against the point. Stay away from the lighthouse and Coast Guard Reservation; visitors are not welcome.

Ocean Beach
County Park

Santa Ynez River

Ocean Park Rd

Surf
Beach

Mesa Rd

**Pacific
Ocean**

Bear Creek Rd

Bear Creek

Coast Rd

**Point
Peder-
nales**

OCEAN BEACH

Ocean Beach Trail

From Ocean Beach County Park to Pt. Pedernales is 7 miles round trip

Ocean Beach County Park

Want to know a military secret? There's a five-mile long beach in the middle of Vandenberg Air Force Base no one knows, where no one goes.

The base, occupying more Southern California coastline than any other private landholder or government agency, encompasses some 35 miles of coastline (about the same amount of shore as Orange County) and public access is severely restricted.

Ocean Beach County Park puts a small part of Vandenberg's beach within reach. Enjoy a walk on a wild and windswept beach and watch for abundant birdlife at the large lagoon at the mouth of the Santa Ynez River.

Speaking of birds, Ocean Beach is prime habitat for the snowy plover, and access can be restricted or the beach even closed entirely from March 1 to the end of September. Oh yeah, the beach is closed during rocket launches, too.

After a visit to the estuary, hit the beach. This walk heads south toward Point Arguello. However, before reaching the point, you'll be stopped by another (Point Pedernales); it's about the end of the public beach. And besides, the surf crashing against the point is nature's way of telling you to turn around.

DIRECTIONS: North of Santa Barbara, just past the Gaviota Pass tunnel, exit Highway 101 onto Highway 1 and proceed toward Lompoc. Join Highway 246 heading west toward Vandenberg and proceed 8 miles out of Lompoc to signed Ocean Park Road. Turn right and drive one mile to Ocean Beach County Park.

THE WALK: Cross the low dunes, dotted with clumps of European beach grass, ice plant and hottentot fig, toward the ocean. You'll pass a couple of pilings sticking out of the sand—the remains of an old fishing pier. Continue over sands, sprinkled with sea rocket and sand verbena to shore. You can walk a mile north on public beach (though the Santa Ynez River mouth can be difficult to ford); this beach hike, however, heads south.

After a mile of walking down-coast, tall cliffs add a dramatic backdrop and splendid feeling of isolation. Atlas ICBMs, Discoverer I, the first polar-orbited satellite, and missiles of all kinds have been launched from Vandenberg.

Look for launch pads and towers as you continue. Ahead lies dramatic Point Arguello, overlooking treacherous waters that have doomed many a ship. One of the worst accidents in U.S. Naval history occurred in 1923 when seven destroyers ran aground in dense fog just north of the point. Officers refused to heed their new-fangled radio equipment or Radio Directional Finder (RDF) stations onshore and instead plotted their course by "dead reckoning" which proved to be dead wrong.

One of the minor reefs of Point Pedernales will stop your forward progress. You might spot harbor seals on the rocks below the point.

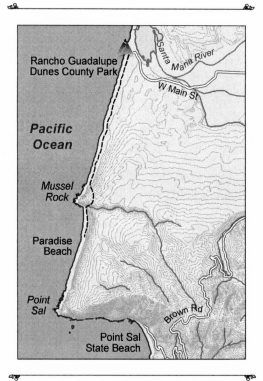

Rancho Guadalupe
Dunes County Park

*Pacific
Ocean*

Santa Maria River

W Main St

*Mussel
Rock*

Paradise
Beach

*Point
Sal*

Point Sal
State Beach

Brown Rd

GUADALUPE DUNES

Guadalupe Dunes Trail

From Rancho Guadalupe County Park to Mussel Rock is 5.5 miles round trip

The Guadalupe Dunes, a magnificent complex of dunes spanning some 18 miles, has to make any California coast-walker's Top Ten List. California's highest and whitest sand dunes are a must-visit visit for their beauty and for the sheer joy to be had in this Sahara-by-the-Sea.

Those towering sand dunes, along with bold cliffs and isolated beaches at the Santa Barbara County/San Luis Obispo County line combine to offer a tableau—and a coastal trek—to remember.

Three miles south of the county-line-marking Santa Maria River is the highest sand dune on the West Coast, 450-foot tall Mussel Rock. It's not really all sand; most of the landmark is a rock formation, though a sand dune lies on top of it.

The beach route, for all intents and purposes, ends at Mussel Rock; hardy hikers can join a rugged unmaintained trail that contours around it. Others might prefer to head inland over the sand dunes or retrace their steps back along the beach.

DIRECTIONS: From Highway 101 in Santa Maria (some 75 miles up-coast from downtown Santa Barbara), exit on Main Street and head west 9 miles to the small town of Guadalupe and a junction with Highway 1. Continue 5 more miles on Main Street to road's end at a beach parking area for Rancho Guadalupe Dunes County Park.

THE WALK: Walk south. In the first mile of your walk, you'll likely encounter the two dominant species of beachgoers in these parts—the surfer trying to catch a big wave and the surf fisherman trying to catch a surf perch or halibut.

After a mile, leave most humans behind, and keep an eye out for some intriguing seashells, particularly sand dollars. A bit more than two miles from the start look inland for a route up into the dunes. Safest and easiest access to, or exit from, the dunes is by way of one of the gulches located a few hundred yards north of Mussel Rock.

(Experienced hikers can continue up to the base of Mussel Rock, scamper up the rock about 30 feet, and join a sandy trail that contours around it. The trail passes above a narrow cove, looks down on a small, wave-battered rock arch, and continues south. Eventually (Mussel Rock is a big rock!) you'll emerge at lovely Paradise Beach, a sand strand that extends from Mussel Rock to Point Sal.)

Coming or going, kids of all ages like walking over the dunes. The lower, shifting sand dunes are dotted with sea rocket, sand verbena and morning glory, while the more stable inland dunes are bedecked with lupine, mock heather and the endangered soft-leaved paintbrush.

The highest dunes are closest to Mussel Rock. Savor the fine coastal views south to Pt. Sal and the 35 miles of pristine coast monopolized by Vandenberg Air Force Base. Northern vistas take in the Guadalupe Dunes, Pismo Beach and the sweep of San Luis Obispo Bay.

JOHN MCKINNEY,
HIKING EXPERT

John McKinney is the author of 30 books about hiking, parklands and nature, including *The Hiker's Way* and *A Walk Along Land's End: Dispatches from the Edge of California on a 1,600-mile hike from Mexico to Oregon.*

HIKE Smart and *HIKE for Health & Fitness* are among the titles in The Trailmaster's Minibuk series, designed to give hikers the information they need in an engaging and easily accessible way.

For 18 years, he wrote a weekly hiking column for the *Los Angeles Times*, and has hiked and enthusiastically described more than ten thousand miles of trail across America and around the world. John, a.k.a.The Trailmaster, has written more than a thousand articles about hiking plus numerous trail guidebooks, including *HIKE Southern California: A Day Hiker's Guide* and *Day Hiker's Guide to California's State Parks.*

A passionate advocate for hiking and our need to reconnect with nature, John McKinney shares his expertise on radio, TV, online, and as a public speaker.

HIKE ON.

www.TheTrailmaster.com